A **Look and Find** Book

DISNEY
PRINCESS

Beauty
and the Beast

 phoenix international publications, inc.

Beautiful Belle lives in a small country village. Her neighbors think she's a bit odd, but Belle doesn't mind. She's interested in her books and her dreams about life out in the big, wide world. This morning she's on her way to the bookshop—again!—as her little town starts a busy day.

Can you spot Belle, local hero Gaston, and these villagers too? Perhaps Belle isn't the oddest inhabitant around...

the bewildered baker

the perfectly paired puppeteer

the milliner's most valued customer

the fun-loving fishmonger

the bemused bookseller

the pig's passenger

Belle's father Maurice has a head full of ideas for new inventions, and a workshop full of strange gadgets, gizmos, and contraptions. Some of them even work! Belle thinks her father is a genius. Sooner or later, he's going to get that wood-chopping machine to chop.

Comb through the clutter to find these irregular inventions:

Personal Page Peruser

Automated Pillow Plumper with 'Choose Your Snooze' Action (patent pending)

Double-Triple Doodad, with (optional) Whizzing Whirligig

Three-Scoop Strolling Seed Sower

Blast-o-Matic Berry Dryer

Press-and-Play Harmonica Helper

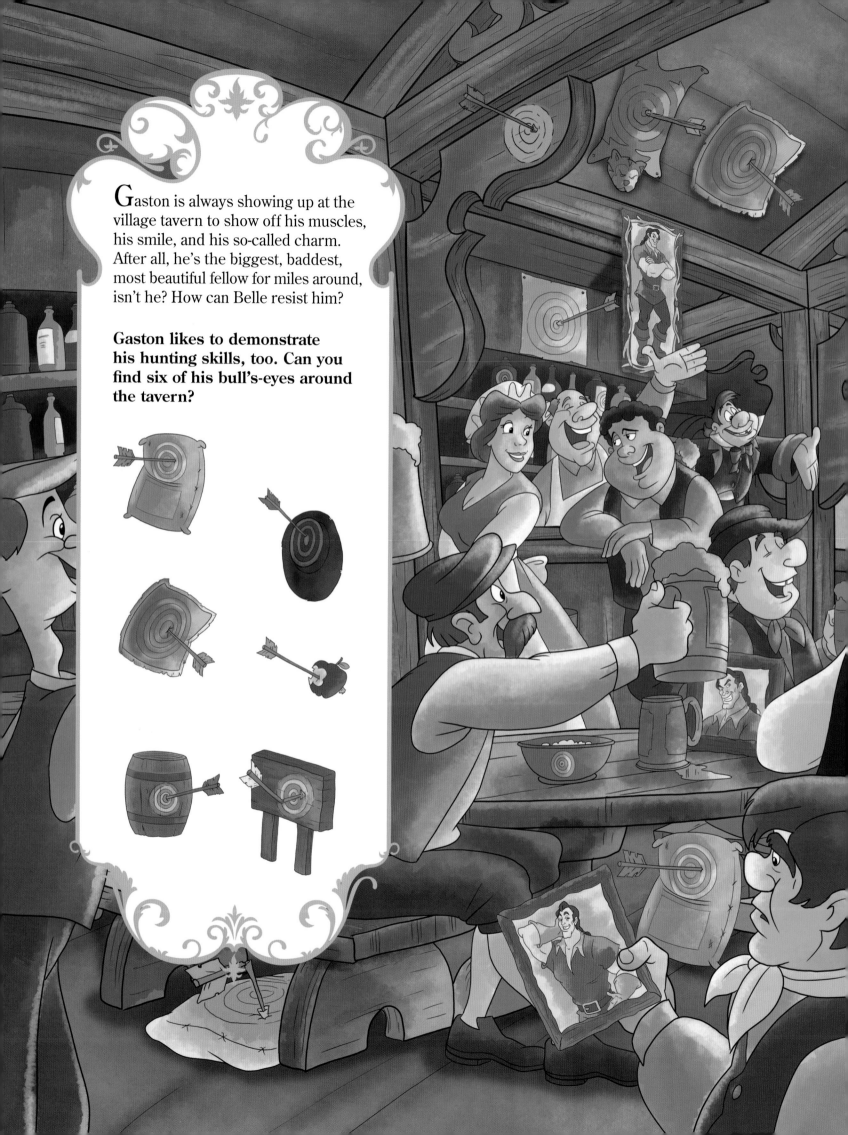

Gaston is always showing up at the village tavern to show off his muscles, his smile, and his so-called charm. After all, he's the biggest, baddest, most beautiful fellow for miles around, isn't he? How can Belle resist him?

Gaston likes to demonstrate his hunting skills, too. Can you find six of his bull's-eyes around the tavern?

When Maurice gets lost and stumbles into a mysterious castle, its master, the Beast, is not amused. Belle agrees to trade her freedom for her father's, and now she's taking her first walk through the halls of this confusing castle.

Join Belle in spotting these things that make her wonder what she's gotten herself into:

a suspicious spider

a perished plant

a scrapped shackle

a colorful coronet

a horned helmet

a Beastly banner

Though the Beast seems chilly and unkind, his servants are determined to make Belle feel at home. Her first dinner in the castle is an extravaganza of skipping spoons, spinning plates, and fantastic food. "Be our guest!" says Lumiere and his friends.

Can you find these tasty tidbits?

a reel-y fresh fish

a sizeable sundae

a prettified pineapple

a feathered fowl

a combustible confection

a cavorting crustacean

Unless the Beast can find someone to love who will love him back, he's doomed to stay a Beast forever. He is beginning to fall in love with Belle…could she feel the same? Perhaps this is the love that will change everything.

Browse around to find these books that can help move the romance forward:

Quell That Curse

Putting Your Best Paw Forward!

Surprise! It's Love!

Make a Second First Impression

Looks Aren't Everything

Speak or Stay Beastly

Beauty: Skin Deep?

When Petals Fall

Dare to Be Different

Make a Second First Impression

Gaston is determined to marry Belle. When he begins to suspect that her feelings for the Beast are standing in his way, he stirs the townsfolk to an attack on the castle. "Rid the village of this beast!" he calls. As the battle rages, Gaston corners his rival on the roof.

Can you find these stony spectators?

Belle rushes to the Beast's side and declares her love. The spell is broken, and the Beast turns back into a prince. Once again, in a tale as old as time, true love has conquered all. Let the celebrations begin!

The Beast's servants are also their true selves again. Can you find the household objects that have replaced them?

Plumette's feather duster

Mrs. Potts's teapot

Sultan's footstool

Cogsworth's clock

Lumiere's candelabra

Chip's teacup

Veer back to the village to find some crazy creatures that also call this place home:

a sausage-loving spaniel

an extremely ambitious bird

a wolf in sheep's clothing

the milliner's horse

a stylish sheep

a cross-eyed cat

Wander back to the workshop to find the first six versions of Maurice's wood-chopping machine. Maybe the seventh time will be the charm?

Gaston has made certain that his favorite hangout displays a few pictures of his favorite person. Turn back to the tavern to find these:

Belle is curious about the castle, and the Beast's servants are curious about her. Hasten back to the hallway to find these hidden helpers:

Chip

Cogsworth

Mrs. Potts

Plumette

Lumiere

Sultan

Belle thinks the servants are sweet to welcome her so warmly. Dash back to the dinner table to find 10 sugar cubes.

The Beast needs to find love before the magical rose upstairs loses all of its petals. Lope back to the library to find these rosy reminders of passing time:

Fly back to the rooftop fray to find these things broken in the battle:

a punched pot

a snapped slingshot

a torn-off tile

a broken blade

an annihilated arrow

a tattered torch

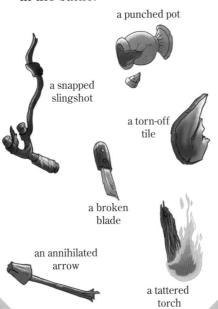

The whole castle is celebrating along with its inhabitants! Bound back to the ballroom to find these symbols of affection: